SUPER
SPORTS TRIVIA

By Jeff Burdick

Gareth Stevens
Publishing

Please visit our website, www.garethstevens.com. For a free color catalog of all our high-quality books, call toll free 1-800-542-2595 or fax 1-877-542-2596.

Library of Congress Cataloging-in-Publication Data

Burdick, Jeff.
Super sports trivia / Jeff Burdick.
      pages cm. — (Ultimate trivia challenge)
Includes index.
ISBN 978-1-4339-8301-6 (pbk.)
ISBN 978-1-4339-8302-3 (6-pack)
ISBN 978-1-4339-8300-9 (library binding)
1. Sports—Miscellanea. I. Title.
GV707.B759 2014
796—dc23

                                    2012047241

First Edition

Published in 2014 by
Gareth Stevens Publishing
111 East 14th Street, Suite 349
New York, NY 10003

Copyright © 2014 Gareth Stevens Publishing

Designer: Andrea Davison-Bartolotta
Editor: Greg Roza

Photo credits: Cover, p. 1 (soccer) Maxisport/Shutterstock.com, (pole vault) Gustavo Miguel Fernandes/Shutterstock.com, (basketball) Shawn Pecor/Shutterstock.com; p. 4 Mike Flippo/Shutterstock.com; pp. 5, 7 (football) Stockbyte/Thinkstock; pp. 6, 7 (scoreboard), 9 courtesy of Wikimedia Commons; p. 8 Heinz Kluetmeier/Sports Illustrated/Getty Images; p. 10 John G. Zimmerman/Sports Illustrated/Getty Images; p. 11 (bottom) Phil Huber/Sports Illustrated/Getty Images; p. 11 (top) John D. McDonough/Sports Illustrated/Getty Images; p. 12 (bottom) Andrew D. Bernstein/Getty Images; pp. 12 (top), 16 (top) PhotoObjects.net/Thinkstock; p. 13 Chuck Solomon/Sports Illustrated/Getty Images; p. 14 (bottom) Vanderlei Almeida/AFP/Getty Images; p. 14 (top) Photodisc/Thinkstock; p. 15 Shaun Botterill/Getty Images; p. 16 (bottom) Transcendental Graphics/Getty Images; p. 17 Bruce Bennett Studios/Getty Images; p. 18 (bottom) Frank Tewkesbury/Express/Getty Images; pp. 18 (top), 29 iStockphoto/Thinkstock; p. 19 Reg Speller/Fox Photos/Getty Images; p. 20 Hulton Archive/Getty Images; pp. 21 (bottom), 22 (bottom) Keystone-France/Gamma-Keystone via Getty Images; p. 21 (top) Aija Lehtonen/Shutterstock.com; p. 22 (top) Bob Thomas/Popperfoto/Getty Images; p. 23 Jamie Squire/Getty Images; p. 24 Ronald Martinez/Getty Images; p. 25 (skier) Allsport UK/Allsport/Getty Images; p. 25 (background) Ezra Shaw/Getty Images; p. 26 Will Hughes/Shutterstock.com; p. 27 (both) David Taylor/Allsport/Getty Images; p. 28 Chlaus Lotscher/Peter Arnold/Getty Images.

Printed in the United States of America

CPSIA compliance information: Batch #CS13GS: For further information contact Gareth Stevens, New York, New York at 1-800-542-2595.

CONTENTS

Words in the glossary appear in **bold** type the first time they are used in the text.

LISTEN UP, SPORTS FANS!

For centuries, people have been coming up with new sports to test the limits of human ability, entertain fans, and just have fun. Some, such as soccer, are team sports that require getting a ball into a goal. Other sports are one-on-one battles between two **athletes**, as with wrestling.

Whether you like the hard-hitting action of football or the skill and grace of tennis, there's a sport out there for everyone. There's a lot of fun sports trivia out there for sports fans, too.

Joining a sport is a great way to stay fit, make friends, and have fun.

FOOTBALL

Who was the first professional football player?

In 1892, the Allegheny Athletic Association football team paid William "Pudge" Heffelfinger $525 to play in a football game against the Pittsburgh Athletic Club.

This made him the first **professional** football player ever! He helped his team win by a score of 4 to 0.

BONUS TRIVIA

Heffelfinger scored the only touchdown in the 1892 game. Today, touchdowns are worth 6 points, but back then, they were only worth 4 points.

Which football team scored the most points in a single game?

In 1916, the Georgia Tech Engineers and Cumberland College Bulldogs played a game in Atlanta, Georgia. Georgia Tech won by the incredible score of 222 to 0! They scored every time they got the ball and racked up a total of 32 touchdowns.

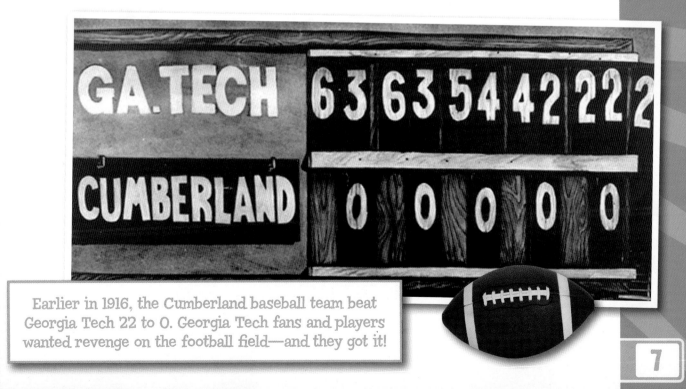

Earlier in 1916, the Cumberland baseball team beat Georgia Tech 22 to 0. Georgia Tech fans and players wanted revenge on the football field—and they got it!

Which team has won the most Super Bowls?

The Super Bowl is the final game for the NFL (National Football League) season. Winning teams are crowned champions of the league for the year. The Pittsburgh Steelers have won six Super Bowls. The Dallas Cowboys and the San Francisco 49ers have each won five.

BONUS TRIVIA

"Super Bowl Sunday" has become a day of feasting for many Americans. It's the second-largest day for eating in the United States, after Thanksgiving.

Quarterback Terry Bradshaw led the Pittsburgh Steelers to four Super Bowl wins in the 1970s.

BASKETBALL

How did basketball get its name?

In basketball, points are scored by throwing the ball through a metal hoop with a net attached to it. However, the first basketball game—played in the Springfield, Massachusetts, YMCA gym in 1891—used a soccer ball and two peach baskets.

This is a photograph of James Naismith, the founder of basketball.

Who scored 100 points in a single professional basketball game?

In 1962, the Philadelphia Warriors beat the New York Knicks 169 to 147—a high-scoring game even for basketball. By far the greatest player of the game was the Warriors' Wilt Chamberlain, who scored an amazing 100 points! This single-game record still stands today and may never be broken.

Chamberlain holds many other NBA records, including the most 50-point games in a row (7) and most points in a single season (4,029).

Who is the tallest athlete ever to play in the NBA (National Basketball Association)?

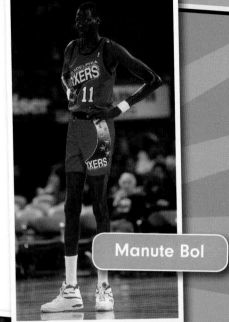

Manute Bol

Two players—both towering over **opponents** at 7 feet 7 inches (231 cm) tall—share this record. Gheorghe Mureșan (George MYUHR-uh-sahn) of Romania played for the Washington Bullets and the New Jersey Nets. Manute Bol (maa-NOOT BOHL) of Sudan played for four different NBA teams.

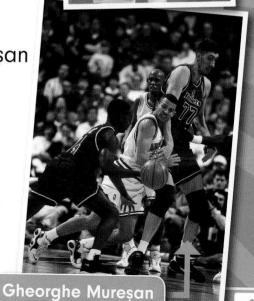

Gheorghe Mureșan

BASEBALL

Who is the best base stealer in the history of professional baseball?

Rickey Henderson stole so many bases during his 24-year career that he was known as the "Man of Steal." Henderson stole a total of 1,406 bases! He also holds the record for most steals in a single season with 130 in 1982.

BONUS TRIVIA

Henderson also holds the career record for most times being put out while trying to steal a base with 335.

Ripkin, nicknamed the "Ironman," played third base and shortstop.

Which baseball player has played the most MLB (Major League Baseball) games in a row?

Cal Ripkin Jr. joined the Baltimore Orioles in 1981. He was named AL (American League) **Rookie** of the Year in 1982. Ripkin spent his entire 21-year career playing for the Orioles. Today, he holds the record for playing in the most **consecutive** games—2,632!

SOCCER

What soccer game had the most spectators in attendance?

The 1950 World Cup Final was held at Maracanã Stadium in Rio de Janeiro, Brazil. In fact, this stadium was originally built for that purpose. Brazil lost the match to Uruguay, 2-1. An astounding 199,854 **spectators** attended the game. Today, the stadium "only" seats about 73,000.

Other major sporting events at Maracanã Stadium include the 2014 World Cup and the 2016 Summer Olympics.

Which player has scored the most goals playing for the US woman's national soccer team?

Mia Hamm played with the US women's national soccer team for 17 years. At age 15, she became the youngest person to play on the national team. At 19, she was the youngest player to win a World Cup. Hamm retired from soccer in 2004 with 158 goals for the US national team.

BONUS TRIVIA

Hamm won two Olympic gold medals playing for the US national team—one in 1996 and one in 2004.

HOCKEY

What is the longest professional hockey game ever played?

During a 1936 NHL (National Hockey League) **playoff** game, the Detroit Red Wings beat the Montreal Maroons 1 to 0 after six **overtime** periods. The game lasted for 176 minutes (nearly 3 hours of playing time), making it the longest NHL game ever played.

Prior to 1959, hockey goalies didn't wear masks.

BONUS TRIVIA

A regular NHL game lasts 60 minutes. So, the 1936 playoff game was nearly the same amount of time as three regular games played one right after the other.

How many NHL players have scored more than 80 goals during a single regular season?

Wayne Gretzky became the first person to score more than 80 goals during the 1981–82 regular season. He scored an astonishing 92 goals! The next season he scored 87. Brett Hull scored 86 during the 1990–91 regular season. Mario Lemieux scored 85 goals during the 1988–89 regular season.

Today, Wayne Gretzky—or "The Great One"—is considered by many to be the greatest hockey player of all time.

TENNIS

Who has won the most Grand Slams in tennis?

A tennis player who earns a "Grand Slam" wins the four major tennis **tournaments** in a single year. Very few players have won more than a single Grand Slam during their career. Australian Margaret Court won three—once in women's singles (1970) and twice in mixed doubles (1963, 1965).

BONUS TRIVIA

Australian Rod Lavar is the only tennis player ever to win two singles Grand Slams (1962, 1969).

Who was the first black tennis player to win a major international tennis tournament?

The four Grand Slam tournaments include the Australian Open, the French Open, Wimbledon, and the US Open. It's a great achievement to win just one of these "majors." In 1956, American Althea Gibson became the first black tennis player to win a major with her singles **victory** at the French Open.

THE OLYMPIC GAMES

When did the first Olympic Games take place?

Ancient records show that the first Olympic Games took place in Greece in 776 BC. They were held to honor the Greek god Zeus. The earliest games only had one event—a 210-yard (192 m) foot race. More events were added later. In AD 393, a Roman emperor declared the Olympics illegal.

BONUS TRIVIA The first modern Olympic Games took place in Athens, Greece, in 1896. First-place winners received a silver medal.

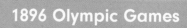

1896 Olympic Games

Who was the only athlete to win a gold medal in both the Summer and the Winter Olympic Games?

At the 1920 Summer Olympic Games in Antwerp, Belgium, US athlete Edward Eagan won a gold medal as a light heavyweight boxer. Twelve years later at the 1932 Winter Olympics in Lake Placid, New York, Eagan won another gold medal with the US four-man **bobsled** team.

Eagan first tried the sport of bobsledding just 3 weeks before winning a gold medal at the 1932 Olympics.

21

Who was the youngest athlete to win an Olympic gold medal? Who was the oldest?

Oscar Swahn

During the 1936 Olympics in Berlin, Germany, 13-year-old American diver Marjorie Gestring won a gold medal, making her the youngest ever to do so. The oldest gold medalist, at 64 years and 280 days old, was Sweden's Oscar Swahn. He won a gold medal for shooting at the 1912 Olympics.

Marjorie Gestring

BONUS TRIVIA

In 1998, 15-year-old American skater Tara Lipinski won a gold medal, making her the youngest gold medalist in the history of the Winter Olympics.

Which city has hosted the most Olympic Games?

Six cities have hosted the Olympic games twice. They include Athens, Greece; Paris, France; Los Angeles, California; Lake Placid, New York; Innsbruck, Austria; and St. Moritz, Switzerland. However, London, United Kingdom, is the only city to host the Olympics three times (1908, 1948, 2012).

Who has won the most Olympic gold medals?

As of 2012, American swimmer Michael Phelps has earned the most Olympic medals. Over the course of three consecutive Summer Olympics (2004, 2008, 2012), Phelps won an amazing 22 medals. Eighteen of these medals were gold—that's twice the number won by the next highest gold-medal winners.

BONUS TRIVIA

Phelps also holds the record for most gold medals at a single Olympics. He won eight gold medals at the 2008 Olympics in Beijing, China.

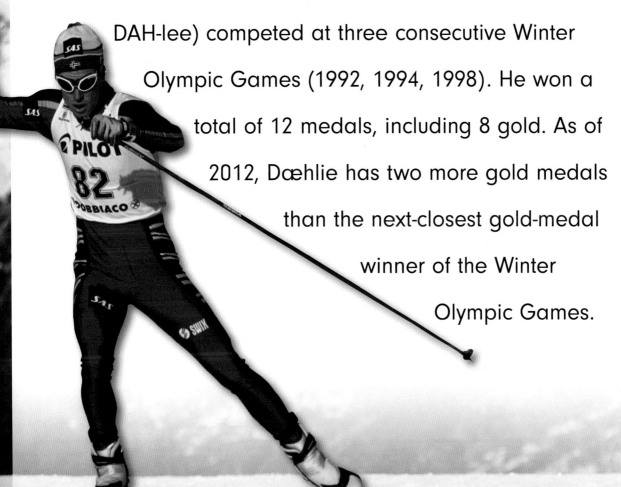

Who has won the most gold medals at the Winter Olympic Games?

Norwegian cross-country skier Bjørn Dæhlie (bee-YORN DAH-lee) competed at three consecutive Winter Olympic Games (1992, 1994, 1998). He won a total of 12 medals, including 8 gold. As of 2012, Dæhlie has two more gold medals than the next-closest gold-medal winner of the Winter Olympic Games.

NOW THAT'S FAST!

What is the fastest moving ball in sports?

Sports fans long believed the fastest ball in sports was the one used in **jai alai**, which has been clocked at 188 miles (303 km) per hour. However, in 2007, Canadian golfer Jack Zuback hit a golf ball that reached a speed of 204 miles (328 km) per hour!

In 1974, 64-year-old golfer Mike Austin hit a golfball 515 yards (471 m)! This record still stands today.

What is the fastest motor sport today?

NASCAR fans love watching race cars speed past at 180 miles (290 km) per hour, but even those machines are no match for a jet-powered car. In 1997, Andy Green of Britain set the land speed record in the Thrust SSC by reaching a speed of 763.04 miles (1,228 km) per hour!

BONUS TRIVIA

As of 2012, the jet-powered Thrust SSC is the only car to travel faster than the speed of sound. "SSC" stands for "supersonic car."

TEAM TIME

What is the oldest team sport?

The oldest team sport was created over 3,500 years ago. The Olmec civilization—which originated in what is now Mexico—played a game with a heavy rubber ball on an I-shaped court. Two teams tried to bounce the ball through a stone hoop using their hips.

Some forms of the Mesoamerican ball game, as it's often called, are still played today.

Become a Sports Trivia Master

From the oldest team game to the fastest modern race cars, there's a lot of cool sports trivia you can use to amaze your friends. But why stop here? Who's the fastest runner on record? Which NHL team has won the Stanley Cup most often? Keep searching for the answers.

GLOSSARY

athlete: someone who is physically fit and takes part in sporting events

bobsled: an enclosed sled for two or four athletes that can be steered

consecutive: following one right after another

jai alai: a court game in which two to four players use long, curved baskets to throw a ball against a wall

opponent: the person or team you must beat to win a game

overtime: an extra period added to a sporting event that ends in a tie

playoff: having to do with games played after the regular season to decide a champion

professional: earning money from an activity that many people do for fun

rookie: a player during his first season in the league

spectator: someone watching a sporting event

tournament: a series of contests testing the skill of many athletes in the same sport

victory: a win over an opponent

FOR MORE INFORMATION

Books

Berman, Len. *The Greatest Moments in Sports: Upsets and Underdogs.* Naperville, IL: Sourcebooks Jabberwocky, 2012.

National Geographic Kids. *5,000 Awesome Facts (About Everything).* Washington, DC: National Geographic, 2012.

Perritano, John. *Big Book of Why.* New York, NY: Time for Kids Books, 2010.

Websites

Official Website of the Olympic Movement
www.olympic.org
Read about Olympic athletes, events, and locations.

Sports Illustrated Kids
www.sikids.org
Stay on top of your favorite sports, see videos and photos, pay games, and much more.

INDEX